Falling *Up*

INTO

WHOLENESS

SELECTED POEMS

Ira Chaleff

2005 – 2020

INVITATION

I am entering an age of disintegration.
Yet, it is also an age of integration.
How is this possible?
Others have explored this phenomenon in prose.
I choose to explore it through poetry.
I invite you to join me in this exploration
that I share with you in my 75th year.

The dandelion does not excuse itself as it is blown apart by the wind. It scatters with the knowledge that it is again merging with the fabric of the wider universe.

Falling Apart Into Wholeness: Collected Poems 2005 - 2020
by Ira Chaleff

ISBN: 978-1-7356288-0-6

Cover design and interior formatting by Yosua Sirait
Dandelion illustration designed by Freepik
Image for cover by Aleksandr Ledogorov at unsplash.com
Image on last page by Pixabay at pexels.com

Printed in the United States of America

ORGANIZING THE POEMS

These poems were written in a zig zag of years between my sixtieth and seventy fifth birthdays. I have organized them in categories that loosely form a progression toward the fullness of consciously accepted death, which invigorates life before letting it go. These are not all the poems written in these years, but the ones curated to comprise a transitional journey. Most of the poems have not previously appeared in anthology, though less than a handful were included in the chapbook, *A Rare Love*, published five years ago as a gift to dear friends, while one tended to the dying of the beloved other.

POEMS

FRAMING THE THEME

Fragile as Grass

Fragile as grass before a prairie fire,
as snow in the cauldron of summer,

these humans, who will be dead
before the cicadas return,

who will be forgotten before
the mountain rises nine centimeters,

whose cultures will be lost
when the seas again cover their lands,

these insignificant specks on specks
in the vastness of the universe,

contemplate the nature of the creator
of all the known and unknown worlds.

How is it they do this if they are not
themselves a lost aspect of the creator?

If some longing in the fabric of creation
is not calling them yearningly home?

If a touch of holy dust
is not forever irritating their throats?

If, like a shadow, they are not
a sign of a stronger presence?

If, like a sacred echo, they are not
returning to the first uttered word?

December, 2010

As I Fall Apart

As I fall apart
may I become whole.

When I was a boy
I dreamed of perfection.

As a man
I long ago abandoned the conceit.

I replaced my aspiration for perfection
with the attainable.

It proving beyond me to heal the world,
I tried to do more good than harm.

Unable to cut a dashing figure,
I dressed my mis-proportions respectably.

Being no genius of the first order,
I would place a strong third.

Unable to be pure of mind and deed,
I was private in my debauchery.

Not graced with transformative love,
I would give love as caringly as I could.

Wealth and fame were elusive,
comfort and achievement sufficed

Pay attention.
These are the formulae for maturity.

Now I've reached the apex.
I am become what I could become.

Next, I enter the decline.
I will unravel in a vaguely predictable sequence.

My heath, my work,
my purse, my comfort.

God willing, my mind will be last
and my love-ties will remain.

As I fall apart
in body, estate and humor,

may the perfection the boy sought
and misunderstood for human

reveal itself in perfect grace
as the soul slips from the ruins.

October 2005

LOVE

Love Notes

I don't write much
about love as it's too hard;
not the writing, but the love.

I do not know where love
goes; it burrows or it hibernates,
could it actually die?

Not just the love between people,
but the capacity itself.
Does it sicken and expire?

All lives must end.
The question is whether this will be
in a blaze of giving glory

or in an exhale of defeat,
worn out by the trying.
Where does love go?

And what is it doing? Preparing
to rebloom or decaying into mulch
for use by other, younger lovers?

These are important questions.
Is love renewable or just recyclable?
And where are recipes

for mixing the renewal elixir?
I would like to write more of Love.
First, I must live more of Love.

I am sure I used to do so.
If you find any notes I made then,
please kiss and forward them to me.

February, 2006

Ecstasy
(The Guitarist)

As the guitarist's fingers tapped the strings
his thoughts, which had been carelessly scattered,
collected themselves and flew in unison
onto the current of rapidly rising chords.

In the micro moment before becoming airborne
he marveled at the power of sounds in their key
to transform his thoughts from prisoners
to escapees, picking gravity's lock.

The rush of his thoughts toward heaven
deprived them of surface oxygen
and they died a swift and natural death
leaving him alone with sudden ecstasy,

which is all his tapping fingers ever craved.

Jan 2006

This Is That Moment

There is that moment in Spring
when the absolute goodness of the world
touches your skin, breezes over your face.

The air is poised at that perfect, fragile balance
between hot and cool, bathing you in
its peace, its comfort, its soothing.

The sweet smell of lilac surfs on the breeze
entering your senses, invading your pleasure centers,
transporting you to times of open childhood.

It is at this moment you form a perfect fit
with that part of the endless universe
in which you find yourself, ecstatically.

In all the moments of our lives,
this is the exceptional moment,
the pure gold coin amongst amalgams.

Our caressed pores open in rapture,
our soul is wrapped in pearl and silk,
our voice rises in silent rhapsody.

This … this… is that moment.

May, 2007

Swirling Around A Center

Two small butterflies
danced wildly around each other
above my head, as I sat
in the warm September sun.

At first, I paid only casual attention
until the dance continued for so long,
with such energetic fluttering,
that a smile opened on my face.

The pair kept their ten centimeter
separation from each other,
never letting the distance grow wider,
swirling around an invisible center.

The smile that insisted itself on me
grew from the conclusion I was witness
to an exuberant mating rite, reminding me
of the everywhere power of Eros.

I craned my neck to track their dance
as the pair rose higher and higher,
always in each other's orbit,
neither pursued nor fleeing.

They danced themselves upwards
until they became lost to my eye
in the sunlight against the sky
and I was left only with my smile.

My smile, and my dreams
of connection and rekindled Eros
in the September of my life,
under the pleasantness of the waning sun.

September 2012

They Read To Each Other

They sit on the beach
reading to each other.
Thirty five years later,
reading to each other.

Their hands touch
as they read to each other.

Thrice parents
twice grandparents
they read to each other.

They sit in the sun
on the beach reading
to each other, while
the world races by.

Nearby, the churchgoers
pray for heaven
while they sit there
reading to each other.

When they read something
special they look up,
and their eyes touch
as they read each other.

When satisfied the other
understands, they look
down to read more.

While their hands touch
their memories touch.
Thirty five years later,
in the sun, near heaven,
they read to each other.

March 2006

BEING

Here

Here, in front of the fire,
logs well stacked, flames licking.
Outside, the old hills
lightly covered with new snow.

Here, in front of the fire
conscious of warmth and beauty,
and outside, of ancient soil
hiding burrows, living and dead.

For a number of days,
it will be me who harbors
this consciousness and keeps
the world appreciated.

Then one day (tomorrow?)
it will no longer be me,
but there will always be another
and another, to carry the mirror

that reflects the world
back on itself, feels the fire,
drinks in the snow, and smiles
at what it sees, living and dead.

February, 2018

Wick Your Tears Gently

Wick your tears gently
with the beauty of sunlight

Dry your anguish
with the softness of clouds

Stifle disappointment
with the first rays of morning

and kindle your spirit
with fire lit new

Ours is the beauty
to envelope old scars

Ours is the music
to soothe what we dread

Today is the measure
of all we may dream

Tomorrow the weighing
of chances afresh

Give thanks for the daylight
revealing the world

Give thanks for the darkness
inviting our rest

We are part of a chorus
singing in praise

Let us sing with great might
what remains of our days.

May, 2012

In Service
To A Higher Beauty

We are all cleaning
the world in service
to a higher beauty.

The old, like me,
wield soft brooms
and light sponges.

The young work outside
clearing fallen logs
and firmly lodged stones.

We clean and repair,
stopping only for sleep
and love making.

Our bodies do the same,
an inward-outward
churning, cleansing.

Our partners, the microbes,
work with the vigor of
invisible swarms and armies.

And what of the cosmic energy
coursing through us in waves
and particles and fields?

This is the world, endlessly
moving, reconfiguring,
converting disorder into pattern.

It is our tyrant and benefactor,
allowing only semi-conscious sleep,
when cleansing must accelerate.

Like the world, we are sand sculptors,
creating order and beauty
until the tide devours our work.

We must laugh and rejoice
in our time to be artists
and holy dung sweepers,

for never was there
a more glorious artistry
than this our world.

We, its voracious despoilers,
are also its preservationists,
curators, patrons and celebrants.

Sweep the studio,
Wash the brushes and chisels,
and be ready for the next sunrise.

April, 2014

Praise The Aesthetic

Praise the useless aesthetic acts of life,
the bed with wine-red pillows on cream counterpane,
the flower arrangement floating on the granite kitchen island,
the vermillion tie matched to the silver gray suit.

Praise the useless aesthetic acts of life
that masquerade as martial pride
in school team uniforms, ecclesiastic robes
and the jaunty caps of bus drivers and trolley conductors.

Praise the useless aesthetic acts of life
that paint lost cave walls,
festoon drab cubicles with children's art
and soften tired doctors' offices and motel rooms.

Praise the tattoos and silver studs,
the music videos and surf board stripes,
the digital photos and sand paintings,
praise them at dawn and at dusk.

Give praise to the time wasted
that could be utilized in the hunt,
monetized in the family economy,
and aggrandized in investment portfolios

Praise the street artist, the busker,
the restaurant designer, altar dressers,
landscapers, zoning boards, picture framers,
window washers and all who help see beauty.

May those acts that do not contribute
to food on our table or dark ink on financial statements,
balance the lopsided scales of utility
with melodies written for the ever-dancing eye.

December, 2006

Traces

Thank you for the traces
of the lives of
old stars and comets
of carbon tested insects,
of poets long gone
and composers' inked scores.

The melodies
and pathways,
the palm-sized tools
and cave paintings
all leave their traces
of the once living.

Thank you for the memories
of ancestors and clans,
of early teachers
and childhood pets,
of favorite stories
and outgrown nightmares.

Where would we be
without the memories
and the records?
Who would we be?
What would be valuable doing
without traces of having been done?

This is the sole reason
for the existence of time,
why the here and the now
are tolerable when given context,
why it makes sense to
record our dreams in the morning

so they can be read
in the long afternoon,
so grandchildren can
pour through diaries
and photo albums
and expired passports.

Even the language-poor
dinosaurs continue to live
through the magnificent record
they have left of their journey.
Even the beetle
and the tiny mollusk.

Thank you for the traces
of old friends on our hearts,
of healed scars from our lovers,
of thoughts and swirls
and old storms, and
peace treaties with ourselves.

Today is another day
to read the record
and decode its writing,
to extol its riches,
enrich its telling, and
plan for its remembrances.

The duty of living
is to discover the secrets
left in traces
by the not-still-living
and to leave our own traces
for the not-yet-living.

Read and record,
lay down and pick up,
marvel and create marvels.
Puzzle maker and breaker,
the giver of thanks and
the reason for future gratitude.

Thank you for the tracer
and the traced, the mystery
and the discernment, the chance
to exist beyond one's existence,
larger than one's footprint,
and longer than this weary day.

February, 2006

IRREVERANCE

What Do You Do?

What do you do?
I put order into life.
How do you do it?
I rearrange deck chairs.
How does that help?
They look better.
Then what?
They shift around.
Do you arrange them again?
Sometimes.
Depending on what?
Lots of things.
Like what?
How my kidneys feel.
What's in my bank account.
My appointments.
Whom I am trying to impress.
Why would they be impressed?
They may not be.
Then why?
So I don't depress them.
Is there anything better to do?
I keep thinking there must be.

Then why keep arranging furniture?
It's here. It's solid.
Isn't time running out?
Yes, it always is.
Concerned?
Too busy arranging chairs.

July, 2010

Did You Know

Did you know it is thought
the moon holds the earth
steady on its axis?

Who holds *you* steady?
(Your axis is showing)

Did you know it is thought
the ability of dogs to smell danger
freed humans from the need of this faculty?

Who warns you of danger?
(You appear to be sweating)

Did you know it is thought
in developing our magnificent brains
we gave up the navigation power of birds?

At times are you lost?
(Please state your migration route to the antipodes)

What pairings allow us to thrive?
What do they cause to wither?
Has a new inventory been scheduled?

When a pairing is severed
we may recover our lost faculties
but sometimes we do not.

What pairings does your inventory reveal?
Do they make you whole
or leave you thirsting?

When we reclaim the capacity to fly solo
we must tolerate the wobbling
despite our motion sickness.

Drinking while flying is not encouraged
(but sometimes it is unavoidable)

You know it is thought
what doesn't kill you
makes you stronger.

Is near-death your personal trainer?
(Now do ten more reps)

June 2010

Ira's Universe

I like Ira.
I like his face,
his virtues,
his foibles.

Just think –
soon he'll be gone!
Just like everyone else.

What's strange
is that when he's gone
he won't know it.

Least not as we reckon.

You see he lives
in Ira's universe
and only sees the others.

So when he's gone
so is his universe.
Poof!

So there's no loss
cause you can't lose something
when it don't have a universe.

Are you following?

Now the question is,
am I also gone?
It don't seem so.

Which is funny
as that means
I'm not Ira.

So then it gets weird
cause who am I then?
And where am I?

Is this me over here?

It's a lot easier
saying it just ends -
when you're gone, you're gone.

It's rational.
It's clean.
It's thinkable.

But is it true?
Or just simpler,
less complicated?

Hard for me to say.

I like Ira.
He thinks a lot.
Maybe too much.

Never shuts off really.
Pain in the ass.
Noisy, chattering bloke.

So when Ira's gone
is the chatterer still here,
or are we free of him?

Chatter, chatter, chatter.

May 2014

Racing Death

I am always racing death,
after all, it is always on my tail.

Can I finish the business of living
before it overtakes and leaves me for dust?

But what is that business?
Tracking filing dates and entrance fees,

or floating love notes and kisses
to those who will miss the glory?

These anxieties haunt me like today's
final judgment passed in court,

which, cowardly, I have missed
and will pay for dearly when awake.

Can I trade in these anxieties
and wrap my arms around your softness?

Around what is pulsing and alive
and affirms my very breath?

Around what is here, not what may go,
or may never be again.

Blessed are the vagabond and minstrel
astride their steeds and wagons.

who bring no weighty baggage
to the by ways they freely travel,

who perform their racy ballads
up tempo, smiling past the final ribbons.

April 2020

Reading The Damn Paper

He was reading the newspaper this morning,
the printed kind, not having quite made the digital transition.

He was reading a columnist who was making
questionable political points; not his best work.

He knew, more or less, this reading was not very important;
that it was mildly recreational at best.

There was a crease in the way he had folded the newsprint
that was obscuring the left margin of the unimportant column.

He dutifully rescored the paper with his thumbnail
to eliminate the crease and reveal the obscured, unimportant words.

The damn paper wouldn't hold the crease and folded back over
    the trivia.
He rescored the page again with his thumb, more deliberately.

The third time the paper flopped over the obscured, unimportant
    words
he became very agitated and began swearing.

This had become a battle over his ability to control the world,
even at this smallest level of detail and frustration.

When his fourth attempt to uncover the unimportant words failed
he became so agitated that his blood pressure spiked hard.

Something, somewhere inside burst and, as he rapidly lost
    consciousness,
he wondered what the fool columnist was trying to prove.

January, 2011

What Is It God?

What is it God?
Why must we deteriorate
the way we do?

If you are benevolent
why don't you whisper in our ear
that it is time for us to go?

Do we need to suffer
in order to be willing
to let go our precious lives?

Must loved ones witness our suffering
in order to accept
the need to let us go?

Surely, you can prepare us gently
by softly chanting meditations,
as a mother prepares her child for sleep.

Your son prepared us through his agony
for the agony that will be ours.
But isn't requiring agony a greater sin than ours?

There are other, gentler ways to purify.
Why do you choose purification by trial?
Where *is* your kindness, your love?

As I bear witness to my friend's dying
I am inclined to believe your universe
has been hijacked by malevolence.

What other conclusion can I reach?
If you are powerful and you are good
are you then asleep at the switch?

Your security arrangements are deficient
to have permitted this hijacking. Wake up!
Or I will need to create a new theory of life

in which you do not have much of a part,
a neutral universe in which
the only love and compassion are ours.

August, 2008

Masterpieces In Melbourne

When I look at the lesser masterpieces
at the Victoria museum
I think how wonderful
that these artists, now dead,
have achieved immortality,
their vision sparkling before my eyes
and entering my delighted mind.

Of course, they have not achieved immortality
as I will die, and so will every other
viewer of their work, and, eventually,
their work itself and the civilization
that is necessary to preserving all of our work.

In the end, therefore,
we are all Zen artists,
creating for the here and now.
The aboriginals who decorated this land
understood the point well –
when you make an intentional mark,
you are stating your existence.

That great philosopher
of our childhood, said it all.
"Kilroy was here." So was I.
So were you.

Australia
circa 2010

WARNINGS

One Day

One day
you wake up
and everything is different.

You feel a lump in your groin,
or your child dies,
or a war destroys your country,
or, or, or.

The trouble is,
you don't know which day
this will be.

All days before this day
are part of an era
that is undefined,
until this day.

You can label the era
"the blissful time"
or "the healthy time"
or "the time of innocent comfort"

but you did not know
it was that time
until it is over.

The future, of course,
is never unknown.
It always ends the same –
in death and decay.

In forgetting
that we know the future,
we live ignorantly
in the present.

The present is the
"here time" and the "now time."
It is the "our time."
and the "dance time."

Even if we have no legs,
even if we have no partner,
even if the music has sour notes.

It is the day before
everything is different.
It is the day to experience

with all our senses,
with sheer, wide-eyed amazement,
the outrageous good fortune
of our time of aliveness!

October 2005

Walking In Shoes

If you walk a mile in my shoes
your feet will hurt.
They are not your shoes.

You may like my smile
and learn something from it.
But the moon deserves your smile.

My life's journey is fascinating,
full of loss and adventures, setbacks
and some victories. So is yours.

My future is limited and unknown,
barely time to tidy up
and try one or two new tumbles.

You may or may not have more time.
My advice: pick a number of years
and dance there in monogrammed slippers.

January 2019

Living With Death

We can't live with the fear of death,
but neither can we live large without it.

The fullness of appreciation billows out
in the gusts of life's fleeting gift.

Like the hummingbird at the Hibiscus,
it owns our attention before darting away.

Like the moon's shadow across the sun,
it will soon pass to others' eyes.

If personal death will be forever,
then we must ravish life today,

tear ourselves from the mundane
and ruthlessly carve space for the sacred.

This is death's message, its warning,
its paradox: Make time for the eternal!

Death is our enemy. Death is our friend.
Open the door and sit together at the table.

When partaking of the final meal,
what is it that requires saying?

Say that in the fullness of love,
and let tomorrow's sunrise surprise you.

May 25, 2020

It Started So Innocently

It started so innocently.
Snow flakes gently arriving,
the walrus' nose
under the igloo flap.

Like any mild rash
it was no cause for concern,
somewhat interesting
in its difference from smooth skin.

How were we to know
that this was a portend,
the exploratory mission
of an invading force?

How were we to know
our curiosity would slowly
turn to anxiety, then alarm,
as the difference developed menace?

The little rash began racing
down your spine
smothering life
in an avalanche of cells.

Our lives, once our own
now belonged to doctors
and lab technicians
and search dogs.

First the volunteers arrived
to shovel the drifts
and offer hot soup
through cracked windows.

Soon they were insufficient.
Snow plows were called in
and utility linemen
and tree cutters with chain saws.

How did these snowflakes
amass an invading army of billions?
How did the few dots on your nape
envelope your organs?

We didn't know then
that the seeds of love and passion
that produced your magnificent mind
and your fine contoured limbs

had spent their vitality
and would succumb swiftly
to the walrus tusks
that pierced into our hearth.

In our innocence
when the storm began
we had no will in place
when the flurries rose to drown you.

February, 2010

AGING

Evening Light

There is a great peace
in going home at evening
when the long shadows of trees
softly cross the road
pointing to golden fields
painted with the day's last light.

When I was young
after I left the home of my birth,
and before I created
the home of my adulthood,
those same shadows
pierced the loneliness of my heart
as I had no home
or knowledge of how to make one.

Now the soft shadows
are of great comfort
reminding me of my journey,
of things I have learned,
have become and created,
now they point home.

In the slanting light of evening
the world appears different,
the sun more beautiful,
as in the slanting light
of my own evening years
the world appears different,
more forgiving, more forgiven,
more like a home.

September, 2007

Stories

I've noticed a change.
I'm too exhausted to
tell my own stories.

They're great stories!
Full of color and energy
and dash and surprise!

But I'm a little tired
of telling them
and hearing myself tell them.

If I tire of telling my stories
who will tell them,
who will remember them?

If I'm tired of telling my stories
and too tired to create new ones,
what footprint will I leave?

If my footprint is fading
on earth, has it begun to appear
somewhere else?

Or are all the stories
dumped into one great
communal story dump

where they are merged
and mashed into
eternal archetypes?

I'm not sure.
I have some thoughts about this.
I have some experiences.

Please, let me tell you
a story about this.
Just one more time.

December 2010

Pointing

Look at the sloppy pointing
in the brickwork of that old house!
Was it done so carelessly at the outset?
Or has time eroded its sharp corners?

Old houses are full of gaps and worn edges
no matter how much those who dwell there
 wish them younger and restored
to their craved and lost perfection.

Or does their perfection include
a design for their demise
so that dwellers do not confuse
these voyaging tents with their destination?

Perhaps the gaps and cracks are roadmaps
that point to invisible treasures at the end
for those willing to take the journey back
to the perfect home, unremembered.

Perhaps the pitted mortar
is becoming sand in the hourglass
reminding us that the perfect beach
was once a million well formed mollusks.

October 2010

When I Had Hair

When I had hair
the world was a little warmer.

I didn't need to keep
a watch cap in my coat pocket

or bring a sleeping cap
when camping under the stars.

I went through many stages
as my hair came in and then out.

One of two birthmarks
was a streak of blond hair

on my forehead
that my mother's friends' envied.

The other was a patch on my chest
that grew fuzz that felt out of place.

One mark was my pride,
one was my shame.

In my twenties and thirties my hair
was an expression of my identity,

worn longish for those times,
with a mustache or curly beard.

After the police called me a dirty hippie
when arresting me at a sit-in

I shaved and had the barber shear me
to give them no excuse to discount me.

Then came the years of the receding hairline
when I fit in better with the power brokers.

Receding led to thinning
until the comb-over became another shame.

I instructed the barber to buzz cut me
to the texture of a summer peach.

My young daughter screamed at first sight,
"You look like a convict!"

She only came to terms when her friends
said, that is how young bald guys do it.

So, I am a youthful old man
whose indispensable possessions

include electric clippers with settings
for numbers "one" and "two" cuts.

My collection of baseball caps for the sun
has grown; my winter hats, too.

I trim the hair that grows irrepressibly
in all the wrong places.

The world is a little colder,
and cutting a fine figure in it more difficult.

But with or without a mane, clean shorn
or stubbly, with pate so shiny

it ruins photos taken with a flash,
I have at least managed to keep my head.

For a once discounted hippie
surely, that is no small feat.

November, 2012

We've Become Old Women

We've become old women,
slow to heal from falls,
with knees that swell
and gimpy ankles and hips.

Our joints are jagged,
no longer smooth
and lubricated
to frolic with secret lovers.

The wear and tear of the tasks
of child rearing, housekeeping,
gardening, stair climbing,
have limited our sexy tango moves.

What art does that leave us?
We can still bat dark eye lashes
and curl the corners of red mouths
in seductive invitation

even if the invitation
is to our salon, not our boudoir,
even if the seduction
is to spirit, not form.

While the light burns behind
our eyes and heats our heart
we can still charm a gasp
from the lips of men.

We can still ignite their
astonished imagination
that creatures as perfect as we
grace their fading existence.

And if the flesh further betrays,
making it difficult to approach us,
we can still laugh in these mangled costumes
 at memories of our youthful premieres.

And if memory betrays us,
making it difficult to focus and orient,
we can still drift into the sweet glory
of the liberation that awaits.

Though our suitors will not see this,
a gifted caregiver from the islands
may notice our ecstasy and whisper gently,
"You go child, you go!"

August, 2012

My Dog Is Old

My dog is old.
She doesn't see well.
She doesn't hear much either.

We find her facing the wall,
not sure what she is doing there,
or where she is supposed to go.

She gets in the way a lot,
standing across the kitchen lanes
or between me and the bathroom,
an inconvenient roadblock.

I nearly run into her fifty times a day.
I get annoyed when I try to move around her
and she moves in the same direction I do.
I snap at her.

I am learning to give her a wider berth,
to be kinder about her failings,
even the trail of stool she leaves in the house.

In human years she is almost a hundred.
With a little luck I will approach her age.
I will need *you* to be kind,
kinder than I have been.
less snappy, more human.

2010

We Are Passing

We are passing.
We are growing thin.
Our ranks are showing holes
that wispy memories only make larger.

We have had a good run.
We have had our share.
Our contributions were not small
even if they were infinitesimal.

There is a parade.
We are somewhere in its midst.
We are all stepping forward
to the point we fall off the edge.

We learned to laugh
at those who thought the world was flat.
Now we know they were right
as those ahead tumble into a void.

We are passing.
We are becoming translucent.
Our hospice nurses are waiting
for us to flash an accepting smile.

We have lead the parade
long enough and far enough.
There are new marshals and drum majors
pushing from the ranks behind us.

Let's wave to the viewing stands.
Let's point upwards to the blue angels.
Is it a Sousa tattoo I hear?
Or a brassy jazz band?

Or is it the sweet lilting pipes?
To whatever I am tuned
let me also be tuned to the
simple strains of gratitude.

I have been in a parade!
What a marvelous parade!
I marched when the sun shone
and when the skies thundered!

And now, now it is time
to thin the foremost ranks
so the clowns and bands and floats
behind us can come forward

waving their unfurled banners,
belting their rhythmic chants,
keeping the spirit of the parade
marching, ever marching.

But until we pass the judges stand,
I , too, will keep on marching
and lift my voice to fill the holes
left by those whom time has taken.

September 2017

When We Are Wise

When we are old and wise
let's sit down under an apple tree
and review the folly of our lives.

Let's laugh at our divorces,
at the bitter arguments we
waged in our finite world.

Let's give them the perspective
approaching death allows
and smoke the pipe of eternal peace.

The universe will soon claim
our memories and transgressions.
Let's offer them up with grace.

There are fewer joys in age
but this great one is in our power,
to laugh generously, heartily at our follies.

June 2007

LOSS

Too Affected By Death

I am too affected by death
especially when it surrounds me.

Why should the death of the
Chinese restaurant owner affect me?

Not just death, even change
has this effect lately.

The sudden removal of the cleaning store
manager leaves me a little bereft.

You see, I told you
I was too affected.

Herschel died this month,
Frank and Alan a couple months earlier,

each a friend of many years.
You see, I told you I was surrounded.

I know the great Buddhist
teaching stories about death,

I aspire to the warrior's exultation,
"Today is a good day to die!"

Even my ego has a certain longing
for the release of ego death.

These are not enough, of course.
I am in mortal combat with these truths.

I read the obituaries, write eulogies,
make appointments with spiritual counselors.

Silly man, so self-centered in a universe
composed of infinite points of life and death.

But this silly man knows
other silly men and women

and he will miss them,
and one day he will be missed.

August, 2008

People Fading Away

I hate watching old people fade away
their voices growing weak
their idiosyncrasies stronger.

I hate seeing the shadow of demise
cross their speech patterns
and mottle their thought structures.

I fear the onset of these shadows
how they will appear
to clients, judges and starlets,
the dismay they will cause my children.

I have written before about Design
the failures and accountabilities
of the Creator, or its minions.

If so, why am I writing about Design again?
Is it the onset, is it the fog
and the clouds distorting my reception?

I hate watching the skin
become thin and brittle
letting the spark leach out.

I hate watching the inevitable
cross the tracks to my side of town
putting me on their wrong side.

There it is!
I hear the whistle blow. I hear
the moan of the approaching dark train.

Where will I bury this hate?
In the eyes? In my sneer?
Alongside the cold tracks?

I hate that I hate.
Is this the proper harvest
of a self-described spiritual life?

As the voice trails off
it is conversion I seek,
a gentler response to the bloody scythe

perhaps grabbing a signal flag
and waving it smartly
as the train crosses the finish line.

January 2006

Bubbles

Ah, we were beautiful bubbles
dancing in the glass of our time!

Was the dance our own effervescence
or that of the freshly poured moment?

We were rousting, we were ribald,
I and my energized friends!

Imperceptibly, the bubbles slowed,
the dance becoming more of a sway.

It still felt like a dance to us
but the youngsters saw us gelling.

We were setting in our own stories,
hardening in our life's plaque.

First slowly, then with greater frequency,
the bubbles began to burst.

A stroke here, a cancer there,
the loss of a mind, the stopping of a heart.

The illusion of prolonged youth at last
could no longer be sustained

and like the individual bubbles
began its terrible bursting,

unendurable, except for the fact
it need only be endured a short while.

April, 2008

My Sister Still Lives

My sister is frozen in time.
Everything she ever did
she did back in frozen time
before the cancer killed her.

Now, she can only relive
in the back-then-moments
that play in my back-then
marvelous-memory-machine.

She lives in the "best of"
trailers that float up,
really "tailers" as they are
only tails of what's left behind.

In the proscenium of my mind
she continues to laugh and vent
but only for me to write about
as she doesn't do interviews.

In the music hall of my mind
she sings protest songs with me
doing the ghostly harmonies
and the insistent parts about justice.

I am grateful that my sister
still lives in some time,
in a rich time. Oh yes,
wasn't that a time!

January 2006

Apology

I want to apologize in advance
to all those who will need to
see me in my decrepitude.
Who will need to tend to me,
to do things I will no longer
be able to do myself.
Personal things, awkward things.

I want to apologize for no longer
being able to sustain the illusion
of being in control that we depend on
to stave off the terror, to quell
the anxiety, to hold off the darkness
with its young nightmares, now returned,
and vague forebodings of what approaches.

I want to apologize and offer
my previous life with you as payment
and the assurance that if it were you
in my place, I would do the same.
Are you not fortunate
that it is not you? Oh, let me add
that I have already done this for others.

With these credentials I will
continue my descent into helplessness
knowing you may need to avoid me
on some days that are difficult,
grateful to see you on others when
you can manage the evidence of chaos,
and, with love, transform its meaning.

April 2008

PREPARING

Dew

Does the dew feel the sun
dissolving her back into air?
Does she mind?

Will we feel the night
dissolving us back into spirit?
Will we mind?

January, 2010

At A Certain Time

At a certain time of day
even a single falling leaf
casts a fleeting shadow
on the ground below.

When I fall
will the sunlight
mark the moment
in hues of gray and black?

At a certain time of life
even a single leaf prepares
to let go its hold, and catch
whatever light remains.

October, 2019

Preparing To Fall

Like a tree
hollowing out
from the center
I am preparing to fall

Like a boulder
on a steep hill
after one rain too many
I am preparing to tumble

Like a cloud
blown too hard
by crosswinds
I am preparing to be scattered

Like a man
tested too long
by small trials
I am preparing to surrender

Like an angel
left to guard
a frail charge
I am preparing to weep

Like a deity
given too much power
and bent with its weight
I am preparing to let go

Like a song
that seeks truth
but loses its way
I am preparing to end

Like chords that progress
in sweet harmony
then risk a jarring discord
I am preparing for their resolution.

August, 2011

Falling Softly

Not paying attention,
I did not see the slick mud.
As I stepped forward, the slide began.
My marvelous gyroscopic instincts
fought furiously to regain my balance
and avoid indignity and welts.

My limbs and torso twisted
this way and that way,
flailing to compensate
for the misstep and imbalance,
for the loss of traction
and the urgent need for stability.

As I flailed, the reality dawned
that all the compensation and urgency,
all the desperate flailing
would not be sufficient
to regain equilibrium and control.
I was going to fall.

At that moment,
accepting the impending fall,
I let go of my resistance,
And focused on falling well.
At that moment, I learned to fall softly,
and softly I fell.

July, 2010

The Witch of December

He feared that the witch of December
would destroy the remains of his soul,

which fought to rise above
the march of his body's decay.

He feared her teeth and nails
and the cold, cold breath.

And so, he resisted and kept her at bay
with firebrands and shards of poetry.

But one day, perhaps when the meadow
lulled him with undulating beauty,

he relaxed his guard and let her approach
until she was close enough to touch him.

As her finger became a silver wand,
grazing the soft hairs on his forearm,

he found himself connecting
to a web of life that was always there,

unseen to his blind eye, unavailable
to the cacophony of his thoughts.

Gently, she stilled his ambitions
and quieted his language,

letting it slip into a primordial
cognition that needs no translation.

As its power suffused him
with her abundant generosity,

he settled into the end of his year.
With ritually cupped hands

he gratefully drank
from the endless living pool,

forever slaking his thirst,
even as December advanced.

November 2017

Burning Candles

I watched two candles burn tonight,
simple white candles, designed for prayer,
not long and tapered for dinner parties
that keep our sense of isolation just at bay.

Circumstances conspired to have me look closely
at these two, their beautifully shaped flames
blue at the base, with golden inverted tear drops
defying gravity and ending in white-hot, nervous tips.

Designed for sacred reflection,
they reached toward heaven,
freeing wisps of gray smoke
they had liberated from solid, earthly form.

Finding myself in the unaccustomed state
of paying full attention,
I marveled at the just-right engineering
that permitted this steady burn without conflagration.

Being designed for prayer, and finding someone
seeking to pray, I saw the lesson before my eyes:
to live life at a controlled burn, hot enough to transform,
cool enough to avoid instant immolation.

I turned my attention away for a moment.
When I refocused, the candles were all but gone,
suddenly losing their equilibrium
and returning to soft, formless pools.

June, 2006

Fading

I awoke with the usual
assortment of stiff muscles
and variegated aches and pains.

But something different occurred,
something like a stranger at the door
with their face contorted against the glass.

For the first time, the virgin time,
I realized one day I will wake and ache
sufficiently, that I no longer care to live.

A shocking thought, a toxic weed
in the summer field where *everything* wants
to live, and fights for the sun and water of life!

Perhaps it is the cumulative effect
of living for months in the age of COVID
without the touch of a human hand,

even the brief touch of a hair dresser,
a phlebotomist, a tai-chi correction, let alone
the touch of a grandchild or a soft beloved.

Yet, I think that is not the true cause,
though perhaps an accelerant. Yes, lack
of touch is a pressurized death accelerant.

But more fundamental, more bedrock,
is that one day, when all comfort has drained,
when gasping can no longer find air,

it will at last be enough to say "enough!"
At that point we begin the frictionless slide,
inviting the relief of death we once hid from.

This taboo, now as thinkable as it is shocking,
could be chronicled as my shameful
collusion with a willing end to Being.

Quick, quick! Let me marshall my defense,
the poet's art of reframing and uplifting,
to reclassify this traitorous thought.

I reframe it as Exquisite Love,
as love for Delight in Life, which,
if lost, willingly loses life itself.

The absence of even a pained delight
offends the animating spirit of the world,
justifying a farewell to that world now past.

There, I've done it! Side-stepped the shame,
assuaged the offended. Now, still here,
I resume fading, slowly and with spirit!

May, 2020

I Have Concluded

I have concluded that
I would rather die suddenly
than suffer a slow unraveling of
flesh and mind endured by man.
Should my preference come to pass,

I need to leave this message
to you, the living, who will
suddenly find me gone from
your life with things unsaid
and certain things undone.

You will be denied the beauty
of the sad surrounding
of my bed in my final hours,
a circle of love and awe
so precious and profound.

I am sorry you will be denied
this final communion, these
last moments to say what
can be said, to plant soft kisses,
to shed sweet tears together.

It is for this reason I write you
this warning, this notice,
that the time for those kisses
and those words of pure love
is today, is every day, is now.

Come hold my hand and
whisper those thoughts
that might otherwise stay
silent in our breasts another
decade, waiting for that circle.

Let me also whisper
those thoughts in your ear,
though the circle hasn't formed,
though evening hasn't fallen,
though the last star hasn't yet appeared.

For I wish you to know
and to carry in your heart
my love for you, my love for life,
my secret knowledge that the terror
of my disappearing forever

is a terror of the flesh,
a terror of the mind,
and not at all a terror of the spirit.
For the spirit will dance,
the spirit will rejoice

at returning to its state
of purest energy,
unencumbered by flesh
that must always deteriorate
regardless of how many

holistic practitioners it employs,
yoga poses it assumes,
blessed herbs it infuses,
aerobic walks it completes
or massages it lets soothe.

When I choose the swiftness
of end, I choose it only if
you let me love you now
and love me in return, knowing that now
 is all we ever have and all we ever had.

November, 2019

DYING

The Terrible Edge

Tonight, I crawled onto the terrible edge
between my life and my death.

We forget its capacity for terrifying us
until we are right there on its razor.

On the one hand there is eternity,
a return of our wisdom to the cosmic pool.

On the other, there is the price of admission,
ego death, the forever loss of who we have been.

It is only when on that liminal edge
that ecstasy and terror become four dimensional.

If only they presented as a choice,
it would still be made with great agony.

Instead, they present as the ultimate extortion.
Why can we not have both,

eternal connection and eternal selfhood?
By what law must we choose?

And by what authority do we forfeit choice
and are forced to accept what is imposed?

I am grateful not to live daily on this edge,
like some more brittle and creative.

To them go the laurels for managing this feat,
and the black roses for their funeral.

There, too, go the saint and the teacher,
but much as they light the way, they are too rare.

For now, I retreat from the edge, perhaps
to better prepare for its awe-full, insistent moment.

April 2020

Can I Die Beautifully?

Can I die as beautifully
as the autumn leaves?

Can I return to the sea
as willingly as the river?

Not so easy my friend,
not so easy.

When we ate the fruit
from the tree of knowledge

we forfeited the innocence
of the river and leaf,

of the snow melt
and the albino deer.

We are burdened by the
awareness of our dissolution

and the universal amnesia
of our face and name.

The snowflake understands
it is immortal in its kind,

the leaf is part of the forest
and content to be its humus.

We have forgotten
what we are part of

that will live as long as
the sap and the river runs.

We have forgotten,
and thus we fear to be forgotten.

November, 2008

Fighting Death

Please do not deny when you are dying,
It does not become your undying soul.

I know you are raging against the bully,
Rage openly, scream your lungs out.

But do not delude yourself with false plans,
Do not deny the anguish of friends sitting with you.

When you are dying, die well
Even as you lived boldly.

Take the fucker death in a headlock
And make him say "Uncle".

Then let him go, shake hands,
and recognize the next round will be his.

Throw an arm over his shoulder
And walk off stage together, drunken buddies.

That grin on your face is your victory.
Death gets the knockout - you win on points.

Yours is the picture we will print in newspapers.
Death always wins, but is nobody's champ.

January 2009

Agony

There's an agony about dying that my poems avoid.
They make dying sound gentle, peaceful.
Sometimes, it is, like idealized love.
More often, it's a bruising donnybrook,
a prolonged, painful punch out
before the final bell rings.

Would that we could all be saints,
beatifically passing to the next plane,
holy men and women, seeing the light
as we ecstatically draw near it,
our eyes peaceful as still water,
our auras caressing those we love.

But many of us will be gasping for air,
fighting our death, struggling,
choking on fluid drowning our lungs,
delirious with toxins we can't void,
punctured by hospital instruments,
or writhing in an accident or an ambush.

It's hard to make poetry from this stuff.
Yet we need to make poetry.
It is poetry that rises from the bloody mess
and lets epitaphs of truthful love
escape from the gravity of decay
and inscribe our head stones with grace.

circa 2009
revised April, 2020

All Creatures Want Comfort

All creatures want comfort
when it is their time to die.
A duckling too small to thrive
curls into itself, as does a starving fox.

People want comfort
when it is their time to die.
My sister brushed her teeth
hours before lolling her head
to the side and exhaling one last time.

My son arranged mats of rubber
and covered them with towels
before lying down in the garage
and taking the poison
that would end his distress.
How do we make our souls comfortable?
My son wrote a brief note:
"I love you - I am sorry"
making a form of peace with those he left.

My sister, lying in bed,
hit a piñata that her sons suspended above her
then raised a fist in victory, declaring
"Not everyone hits a piñata the day they die!"

Many are unable to find comfort
until a physician increases the morphine
"to calm the panic" of insufficient oxygen
or to calm the gathered family
witnessing the agony of departure's labor.

How will we comfort ourselves at death's moment?
What will be our piñata and our rubber mat?
Who will we reach out to as consciousness fades,
to curl up in their love, to warm ourselves in their light?

January 3, 2010
My son's birthday

There Is Something To Do

There is something I am supposed to do,
though I don't know what it is.
Am I to write my children?
Leave notes in unexpected places?

There is something I am supposed to do.
I feel the spirit whispering in me.
But what? Say goodbye to old friends?
Unearth the gold I have hidden, where?

Am I to rush into the public space,
and like an Indian warrior of yore,
bind my leg to a stake in the ground
and cry one more time for justice?

Am I to quiet my heart and thoughts,
find the sitting ground on mother earth
and let the waves of peace flow,
known only to those fully present?

This is the price paid for freedom.
I have lost the wisdom that guided
my ancestors along marked paths
in the transition required of all living souls.

I sit here, short of full peace,
as I search for a channel to the well
that flows deep within the rock
that anchors my receding life.

I shuffle into a comfortable position
in which I can wait, trusting that
what I am to do, will reveal itself
when it is time to follow the calling.

April, 2020

Whose Faces?

Whose faces will surround my bed
when I at last lay dying?

Whose moist eyes will attend me,
and slight smile send me bravely on?

Life, so strange, should have
long clarified this importance,

yet it shifts in unpredicted,
indeterminable ways.

The eyes will be those who are nearest,
present to the unplanned hour.

The hands holding my hands
will be the hands of those who are left,

who have not been mowed down by time,
nor driven away by love's twists.

The hearts will be those who care,
whether that care be recently formed

or the tapering residue
of a lifetime's friendship.

The smiles, I pray, will be those of eternal spirit,
shining through the circle of embodied souls.

Let me hear a laugh of knowing,
as the last step here precedes the first elsewhere.

Let the tender farewell kiss be prelude
to the ecstatic peace awaiting.

November, 2010

Fall Where You Make A Difference

Sometimes a tree must fall
into the river, to form a disturbance
in the water that flows over it
with the beautiful sound of a cascade.

Sometimes a man must fall
in the flow of his time
to disturb its complacency,
creating the beautiful sound of justice.

If you can, fall where you will
make a difference, and a sound
that will be long and beautifully heard
by those who pass by that sacred place.

February, 2006

No Good Point

There is no good point
to end a book of poems
about dying, short of dying.

As in ending life,
we attempt to
do so gracefully.

As in living life, we often
do not fully succeed,
but we try to come close.

For a not unsuccessful life
an epitaph might read,
"He came close enough."

January, 2011

Today Is The Day

Put on your brave face
Your dying face
Today is the day.

All your life
You have prepared
Today is the day.

Put on your brave face
Your spirited face
Today you are the teacher.

All your loved ones
Have gathered around
Today is the day.

Those you love are struggling
To put on their brave face
Their spirited face.

Today is the day
To help those you love
Accept your farewell.

Put on your loving face
Your wondrous face
Today is the day

When all becomes dark
When all becomes light
Today is the final day

Or the first day
Or the no day
Or the eternal day.

Put on your brave face
Your loving face
Your gift face to the world.

Today is the day
That you leave us
Our final memory

Our spirited memory
Our loving memory
Our indelible memory.

Today is the brave day
Now is the love hour
This is the moment

Between earth time
And eternity
This is the brave time.

December, 2005

Now I Am Ready

The night grows quiet,
the tree frogs are hushed,
the air is as still as eternity.

My breath grows quiet,
synchronizing with the stillness
that moves neither in nor out.

If I ever knew such peace in life
I would have walked more lightly;
now I repose gently in its embrace.

I am rocked by a mother whom I
cannot see, whose arms enfold me
until I am soothed, ready to let her go.

Now I am ready.

August 2015
Revised April 2020

AFTERTHOUGHT

Wholeness

Wholeness is not perfection.

It is the emerging patterns
and the unarranged parts
seeking their completion.
It is touching them softly,
to better map our understanding.

As I fall apart,
I turn to these patterns
and lift them with the language
currently available to me,
aware there are many tongues
and an infinity of lived dialects.

I offer you a codex
in which these patterns are examined.
I invite you to explore the words
that reside within you.
Together, we may yet discern
the wholeness of our ripening evolution.

April, 2020